Collins

easy lea

Spelling

Ages 8-9

How to use this book

- Find a quiet, comfortable place to work, away from distractions.
- Tackle one topic at a time.
- Help with reading the instructions where necessary, and ensure that your child understands what to do.
- Help and encourage your child to check their own answers as they complete each activity.
- Discuss with your child what they have learnt.
- Let your child return to their favourite pages once they have been completed, to talk about the activities.
- Reward your child with plenty of praise and encouragement.

Special features

- Yellow boxes: Introduce a topic and outline the key spelling ideas.
- Red boxes: Emphasize a rule relating to the topic.
- Suggests when your child can use a dictionary to help with the spelling or understanding of a word.
- Orange shaded boxes: Suggest activities and encourage discussion with your child about what they have learnt.

Published by Collins
An imprint of HarperCollins*Publishers*
1 London Bridge Street
London SE1 9GF

Browse the complete Collins catalogue at
www.collins.co.uk

© HarperCollins*Publishers* 2015

10 9 8

ISBN 978-0-00-813443-3

The author asserts her moral right to be identified as the author of this work.

The author and publisher are grateful to the copyright holders for permission to use the quoted materials and images.

p5 © Nearbirds/shutterstock.com,
© TheBlackRhino/shutterstock.com;
p7 © Fernando Eusebio/shutterstock.com;
p25 © AnastasiaSonne/shutterstock.com;
p31 © sundatoon/shutterstock.com

All rights reserved. No part of this publication may be reproduced, stored in a retrieval system, or transmitted, in any form or by any means, electronic, mechanical, photocopying, recording or otherwise, without the prior permission of Collins.

British Library Cataloguing in Publication Data

A Catalogue record for this publication is available from the British Library

Written by Rachel Grant
Page design by QBS Learning
Cover design by Sarah Duxbury and Paul Oates
Cover illustration by Kathy Baxendale
Project managed by Andy Slater

Printed and bound in Great Britain by
Bell and Bain Ltd, Glasgow

Contents

'ch' words	4
More 'ch' words	5
Prefixes 're' and 'pre'	6
Prefixes 'aero', 'aqua' and 'tele'	7
Prefixes 'inter', 'micro' and 'sub'	8
Possessive apostrophe with plural words	9
Letter pattern 'sc'	10
Words with 'ey', 'ei' and 'eigh'	11
Words ending 'ice' and 'ise'	12
Homophones	13
Words ending 'able' and 'ible'	14
Words ending 'ably' and 'ibly'	15
Suffixes that start with a vowel	16
Compound words	17
Prefixes 'co' and 'ex'	18
Suffix 'ly'	19
Words ending 'ally'	20
Near homophones	21
Words with 'ough' and 'augh'	22
More suffixes that start with a vowel	23
Root words and word families	24
Suffix 'ous'	25
Words ending 'ious' and 'eous'	26
Words ending 'sion' and 'tion'	27
Prefixes 'bi', 'semi', 'tri' and 'oct'	28
Words ending 'ssion' and 'cian'	29
Word ending 'cious' and 'tious'	30
Tricky words	31
Answers	32

'ch' words

Say these words out loud. Listen to the sound of **ch**.
The **ch** in school sounds like the letter **k**.

children   s**ch**ool

Words with a **ch** that sounds like **k** often come from the Greek language.

1 What am I? Work out the answers to these clues.
The answers are all words with **ch**.

I lay eggs. _____

I am a place children go to learn. _____

I'm made of bread and people eat me for lunch. _____

I am a group of people who sing. _____

2 Sort these words by the sound of **ch**.

chocolate   research   technology   change   chemist   orchestra

ch as in stoma**ch**	**ch** as in **ch**in

3 Write three nouns that have a **ch** like in school. Try to think of words that are not on this page. Then write the plural of each word.

_____   _____   _____

_____   _____   _____

More 'ch' words

Say these words out loud. Listen to the sound of **ch**.
The **ch** in chalet sounds like **sh**.

chalet   an**ch**or

Words with a **ch** that sounds like **sh** often come from the French language.

1 Sort these words by the sound of **ch**.

machine   ache   brochure   echo   scheme   chef

ch as in **ch**emistry	**ch** as in **ch**alet

2 Work out the answers to these clues. The answers all have a **ch** like in chalet.

Someone whose job is to drive people around. _____

Used to slow down something that is falling. _____

A strip of hair grown above a man's top lip. _____

A person who cooks for a living. _____

A pie without a top made mainly from eggs. _____

3 Choose two words from question 1 that have **ch** as in chalet. Write them in two short sentences.

_____

_____

With your child, make a list of words with different **ch** sounds. Discuss the meaning of each word.

Prefixes 're' and 'pre'

re and **pre** are **prefixes**.

repaint   **re** means **again** or **back**.

predict   **pre** means **before**.

1 Draw a line to match each word with its meaning.

- refresh — to arrange something in advance
- return — belonging to a time before written history
- prearrange — to give new strength or energy
- prehistoric — to put something back or to change something
- replace — to come or go back to a place
- preschool — a nursery or kindergarten

2 To which words can you add both **re** and **pre** to make two new words? Write the new words beneath.

present   heat   school   test   pay   pare   book

_____ _____ _____ _____

_____ _____ _____ _____

3 Think of other words that start with **re** or **pre**. Write them in the box.

Explain to your child that sometimes hyphens are used to join a prefix to another word. We use a hyphen to avoid confusion between two words with different meanings, for example, re-cover (to cover again) and recover (to return to health). With your child, look up similar examples in a dictionary.

Prefixes 'aero', 'aqua' and 'tele'

aero, **aqua** and **tele** are prefixes.

aeroplane   **aero** means **air**.
aquaplane   **aqua** means **water**.
telescope   **tele** means **far off** or **distant**.

1   Add **aero**, **aqua** or **tele** to complete these words.

_____plane   _____space   _____phone   _____graph

2   Write each of these words in a sentence.

aquarium _____

aerosol _____

television _____

aerobics _____

telephone _____

3   Write your own definition for each of these words. Look at the meaning of each prefix.

aerodrome _____

aqualung _____

telescope _____

Prefixes 'inter', 'micro' and 'sub'

inter, **micro** and **sub** are prefixes.

internet   **inter** means **among** or **between**.

microwave   **micro** means **small**.

submarine   **sub** means **under** or **below**.

1 Complete the sentences using words from the box. You will have two words left over.

| international   microscope   subheadings   interview   subway |

Ali's _____ was successful. He got the job!

_____ help you to find information quickly in a book.

To see the tiny insect through the _____ was amazing.

2 Write a word using each prefix. Put each word into a sentence.

inter_____   micro_____   sub_____

_____

_____

_____

3 Are these real words? Tick (✓) the correct words and cross (✗) the incorrect words.

     interscope   microchip   subterranean

     microsect   intersect   subreact

Ensure that your child understands the meaning of each prefix and how it changes the meaning of a word.

Possessive apostrophe with plural words

To show possession with plural words, put the apostrophe after the plural form.

> If the plural ends in **s**, do not add another **s**.   boys   boys'
>
> If the plural does **not** end in **s**, add **s**.   children   children**'s**

Take care with proper nouns, such as people's names. If a word ends in **ch**, **s**, **x** or **z**, add the apostrophe to the plural form.
the Birches' dog = the dog belonging to the Birch family.

1 Read each sentence. Then write the missing word.

The territory where lynxes live.   The _____ territory.

The daughters of Mrs Henderson.   Mrs _____ daughters.

The house where the Jensens live.   The _____ house.

2 Circle the correct form for each proper noun in these sentences. The singular proper noun is in brackets.

Tim loves spending time at the **Finches / Finches' / Finch's** house. (Finch)

The **Sanchez / Sanchez's / Sanchezes** are going on holiday. (Sanchez)

3 Write a short possessive sentence using the plural of each of these nouns.

child _____

parent _____

woman _____

Work through the rules on this page with your child. Encourage your child to find more examples of apostrophes used for possession in their reading book and in the world around them, for example, in shop names. Look for any that you think may have the apostrophe in the wrong place.

Letter pattern 'sc'

The letter pattern **sc** can make different sounds in words. Sometimes the **c** is silent. Say the following words out loud.

science　　　de**sc**end　　　tele**sc**ope　　　**sc**are

Many words with **sc** and silent **c** come from the Latin language.

1 Complete these sentences using **sc** words from the ribbon.

We used _____ to cut out the paper dolls.

It was a difficult _____ experiment.

Why do stars and the sky _____ us so much?

Most climbers attempt to _____ Mount Everest during April and May.

It takes a lot of _____ to do your homework every night.

Ribbon words: discipline, ascend, scissors, fascinate, scientific

2 Sort these **sc** words by the sound they make.

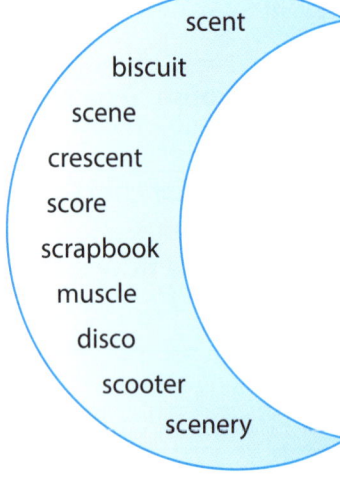

scent, biscuit, scene, crescent, score, scrapbook, muscle, disco, scooter, scenery

sc as in scare	sc as in science

3 Write these words in sentences.

fascinate _____

scene _____

Words with 'ey', 'ei' and 'eigh'

The long vowel sound **ay** can be spelt in different ways.

Say these words out loud.

th**ey**   v**ei**n   **eigh**t

Only a few words use **ey, ei** and **eigh** to spell the **ay**, sound.
They are common words, so you need to learn how to spell them.

1 Add **ey, ei** or **eigh** to make a word.

gr_____   r_____ns   n_____bour

surv_____   ob_____   w_____t

2 Some of these **ey, ei** and **eigh** words have been spelt incorrectly. Tick (✓) the correct words and cross (✗) the incorrect words. Write out the correct spellings for any you have crossed.

convey ☐   freight ☐   wiegh ☐

vayl ☐   eyty ☐   preigh ☐

neigh ☐   sleigh ☐   grey ☐

_____   _____   _____

3 Think of more words with the **ay** sound. Write them in the box.

Be sure your child understands that the same sound can be made by different spellings. Try creating **ay** words from the letters in car registration numbers. For example, VN ... could produce vein, ET... could produce eight, PY... could produce pray.

Words ending 'ice' and 'ise'

Some words ending **ice** and **ise** sound the same, others sound different

prac**tice**   prac**tise**
ad**vice**   ad**vise**
de**vice**   de**vise**

1 Complete the sentences using the words from the box.

exercise   office   realise   surprise

To get fit, eat healthily and take plenty of _____.

The birthday party was a big _____.

I did not _____ you had a brother.

The headmaster will see you in his _____.

2 Write each of these words in a sentence.

advise _____

advice _____

practise _____

practice _____

3 Circle the word in each pair that is spelt correctly.

paradise   paradice

cowardice   cowardise

polise   police

justise   justice

organice   organise

recognice   recognise

A mnemonic is a way to make it easier to remember information. Encourage your child to come up with a mnemonic to remember which spelling is usually a noun and which a verb, for example, 'ice' is a slippery noun, 'ise' is not a noun.

Homophones

Homophones are words that sound alike but are spelt differently and have different meanings.

flour   flower

1 Can you work out the homophone pairs from these clues?
Write the words in the spaces. The first one has been done for you.

| beef, lamb, chicken | see someone for the first time | meat | meet |

| two things that belong together | a fruit | _____ | _____ |

| a rabbit-like animal | it grows on your head | _____ | _____ |

| to look | the ocean | _____ | _____ |

| cats' feet | to stop for a moment | _____ | _____ |

2 Write a homophone for each word. Then write a sentence using **one** of each pair.

mane _____ _____

whether _____ _____

steak _____ _____

whose _____ _____

3 Write two homophones for each of these words.

there _____ _____   rain _____ _____

heel _____ _____   seize _____ _____

If your child is confusing particular pairs of homophones, make sure they clearly understand the different meanings of each word and then provide opportunities for them to use the words correctly in their writing.

Words ending 'able' and 'ible'

Some words end in **able** and **ible**.

cap**able**   ed**ible**

Many words that end in **ible** come from the Latin language.

If you remove **able** from a word you are often left with a complete word.   like**able**
If you remove **ible** from a word you are often left with an incomplete word.   incred**ible**
Take care! There are many exceptions, such as:
avail**able**   navig**able**   cap**able**   flex**ible**   suggest**ible**   resist**ible**

1 Add **able** or **ible** to complete these words.

comfort_____   terr_____   reason_____   sens_____

vis_____   flex_____   accept_____   poss_____

2 Write each of these words in a sentence.

horrible   _____

dependable   _____

desirable   _____

legible   _____

3 Complete these sentences by circling the word that makes sense.

Our meal was completely **valuable** / **inedible** / **comfortable** / **reliable**.

We need a delivery driver who is **valuable** / **inedible** / **comfortable** / **reliable**.

Your home is very **valuable** / **inedible** / **comfortable** / **reliable**.

That vase must be very **valuable** / **inedible** / **comfortable** / **reliable**.

With your child, look for **ibly** and **ably** words in their reading book. Notice that **able/ably** endings are more common than **ible/ibly** endings. If **ably** is added to a word that ends in **ce** or **ge**, the **e** after the **c** or **g** is kept so that the letter keeps its soft sound (e.g. notice/noticeably).

Words ending 'ably' and 'ibly'

Some words end in **ably** and **ibly**.

suit**ably**   lov**ably**   unbear**ably**   vis**ibly**   imposs**ibly**   forc**ibly**

Many words that end in **ibly** come from the Latin language.

1 Circle the four **ably** and four **ibly** words in this word search.

l	e	g	i	b	l	y	r	b	l	e	y
a	n	y	s	e	n	s	i	b	l	y	o
c	o	n	s	i	d	e	r	a	b	l	y
p	r	a	d	o	r	a	b	l	y	l	g
v	t	e	r	r	i	b	l	y	n	b	t
n	o	t	i	c	e	a	b	l	y	c	s
c	o	m	f	o	r	t	a	b	l	y	y
b	t	f	l	e	x	i	b	l	y	u	m

2 Choose three of the words from the word search. Write each one in a short sentence.

_____

_____

_____

3 Use these words to complete the sentences.

considerably   responsibly   comfortably   reasonably

Please behave _____ when you are on the school bus.

We have now settled _____ into our new flat.

Your spelling has improved _____. Well done!

We are _____ confident that we will win this match.

15

Suffixes that start with a vowel

Adding a **suffix** to a word changes its meaning. Some suffixes start with a vowel, for example, **ing**, **er**, **ed**, **ation**. Use these rules for words with more than one syllable.

> If the **last** syllable is **stressed** and ends with one consonant, **double** the final consonant. forg**et** (**et** is **stressed**) forg**etting**
>
> If the last syllable is **not stressed** and ends with one consonant, **do not double** the final consonant. gard**en** (**en** is **not stressed**) gard**ening**
>
> Take care! There are two common exceptions to this rule:
> trav**el**   trav**elling**   canc**el**   canc**elled**

1 Complete these word sums. Check your finished words in a dictionary.

limit + ing _____   begin + er _____

prefer + ed _____   limit + ation _____

offer + ed _____   permit + ed _____

upset + ing _____   travel + ed _____

2 Put a cross next to the words that are spelt incorrectly. Write them correctly.

| quartered | happenning | canceled | appearing |
| jeweler | worshipped | woollen | fullfiled |

_____ _____ _____ _____

3 Write two sentences using both words in each pair.

   gardener   gardening   traveller   travelled

_____

_____

If your child has difficulty with doubling consonants when adding a vowel suffix, make sure they can hear where the stress is falling in the root word – on the first syllable (e.g. garden) or the second (e.g. forget).

Compound words

A compound word is made from two words put together.

sand + castle = sandcastle

1 Finish the compound words with words from the sun.

words on sun: noon, drop, light, shake, head, case

over_____   rain_____   after_____

sun_____   pillow_____   hand_____

2 Draw lines between the two sets of words to create compound words.

back   house   meat   news   play   pass

letter   up   word   ground   hold   balls

3 Write three compound words using each of these words.

bath   _____   _____   _____

cross   _____   _____   _____

home   _____   _____   _____

With your child look for examples of new compound words that are being created as the language changes and develops, especially technological words, for example, voicemail.

Prefixes 'co' and 'ex'

co and **ex** are prefixes.

cooperate — **co** means **joint** or **together**.

express — **ex** means **out of** or **from**.

1. Add the prefix **co** or **ex** to these words.

_____it   _____change   _____incidence

_____ordinate   _____port   _____claim

2. Write the correct word for each definition using words from the box.

> cooperate   extract   coeducation   express   coincidence   exclude

When boys and girls are taught together in the same school. _____

To state something clearly. _____

To work willingly with others to do something. _____

To take out or remove. _____

To leave out. _____

Linked events that are not planned but seem like they are. _____

3. Write each of these words in a short sentence.

cooperate _____

express _____

Explain to your child that some **co** words can be spelt with or without a hyphen to join the **co** prefix to another word, especially if the root word begins with a vowel (e.g. co-ordinate, co-operate).

Suffix 'ly'

ly is a suffix. Add **ly** to an adjective to make an adverb.

quick   quick**ly**   dangerous   dangerous**ly**

It's the same for adjectives ending in **l**.

usua**l**   usua**lly**   hopefu**l**   hopefu**lly**

An adjective that ends 'consonant + **le**': remove the **le** then add **ly**.

sim**ple**   sim**ply**

An adjective that ends 'vowel + **le**': add **ly**.

ag**ile**   agile**ly**

Take care with these exceptions:

true   tru**ly**   due   du**ly**   whole   who**lly**

---

1 Add **ly** to these adjectives to make adverbs.

probable _____   possible _____   wise _____

reasonable _____   whole _____   awful _____

2 Complete the second sentence by writing in the correct adverb.

Jim is a courageous football player.   Jim plays football _____.

Slice the cheese as thinly as possible.   Slice it as thinly as you _____ can.

He is humble about his achievements.   He talks _____ about them.

Mum paid the bill when it was due.   The bill was _____ paid.

3 Write each of these words in a sentence.

favourably _____

simply _____

Words ending 'ally'

The suffix **ly** changes an adjective into an adverb.

When **ly** is added to a word that ends in **c**, add **al** before the **ly**.

comi**c**   comi**cally**

There is one exception to this rule: publ**ic**   publ**icly**

1 Add **ly** to these adjectives to make adverbs. Be careful how you spell each one.

Adjective	Adverb	Adjective	Adverb
basic		athletic	
occasional		historic	
frantic		accidental	
public		automatic	

2 Complete these sentences using words from the box.

automatically   optimistically   dramatically

This camera adjusts itself _____.

If you learn your lines, your performance will improve _____!

'I think the weather will be better tomorrow,' she said, _____.

3 Write two words ending in **ally**. Write each word in a short sentence.

_____ _____

_____ _____

Ensure that your child learns the spelling rules in this topic as well as those on page 20.

Near homophones

Homophones are words that sound alike but have different meanings and spellings.

Near homophones don't sound **exactly** the same but they sound similar enough for people to confuse them.

affect – usually a verb   effect – usually a noun

1 In each pair of words is a noun and a verb. Circle the noun and underline the verb.

practice   practise   licence   license   advise   advice

2 Choose the correct near homophone from each pair to complete each sentence.

grandma grammar   advice advise   lose loose   affect effect

Make sure you wear _____ fitting clothes for dance practice.

'I _____ you to brush your teeth at least twice a day', the dentist said.

Always check your writing for spelling, _____ and punctuation errors.

The new English teacher has had an amazing _____ on our class.

3 Choose one of these pairs of near homophones and write a sentence for each word. Then think about sentences you could write for the other words.

admit omit   woman women   accept except

_____

_____

With your child, think of other near homophones that are often confused. Look up the meanings of the words in a dictionary and then ask your child to think of a sentence that uses each word.

Words with 'ough' and 'augh'

Some words end in **ough** and **augh**. They are pronounced in many different ways.
Say the words below and listen to the sounds **ough** and **augh** can make.

tr**ough** (**off** sound)   th**ough**t (**aw** sound)
r**ough** (**uff** sound)   pl**ough** (**ow** sound)
th**ough** (**oh** sound)   c**augh**t (**aw** sound)

1 Sort these **ough** words according to the sounds they make.

| dough | cough | although | trough | tough |
| taught | bough | drought | ought | enough |

aw sound	**uff** sound	**ow** sound	**oh** sound	**off** sound

2 The underlined words in the sentences have been spelt as they sound. Write the correct spellings underneath each sentence.

Thow the troff was deep, I thort the horse wouldn't have enuff to drink.

_____   _____   _____   _____

We fawt hard against the ruff, tuff team and, sure enuff, we won!

_____   _____   _____   _____

Maria cawt a terrible cold so I bort her some coff sweets.

_____   _____   _____

3 Write an **ough** or **augh** word for each **aw**, **ow** and **uff** sound. Use words that are not on this page.

aw _____   ow _____   uff _____

More suffixes that start with a vowel

As we have seen, some suffixes start with a **vowel**, for example, **ing**, **er**, **ed**, **ence** and **ance**.

When you add a suffix to a word ending in **fer**, for example, **refer**, say the word out loud.
If **fer** is still **stressed** after the suffix is added, you need to **double** the r.   re**ferr**ed
If **fer** is **not stressed** after the suffix is added, you do **not double** the r.   re**fer**ence

1 Complete these word sums. Make sure you spell the finished words correctly.

forget + ing _____   transfer + ed _____

admit + ance _____   upset + ing _____

suffer + ed _____   occur + ence _____

2 Add **ed** and **ence** to each of these words to make two new words.

refer _____   _____

differ _____   _____

prefer _____   _____

confer _____   _____

3 Write each of these words in a sentence.

preferred _____

difference _____

transferring _____

Root words and word families

A **root word** is a word that can have prefixes or suffixes added to it.

move

A **word family** is a group of words that share the same root word.

re**move**   **mov**ement   **mov**ing   un**mov**ed   re**mov**al

1 Work out each root word and the meaning shared by each word family. Circle the root word and write the meaning for each one.
The meaning can be just one word.

hydrant	pedicure	dictation	thermostat
hydrate	pedal	verdict	thermometer
dehydrate	pedestrian	diction	thermos

Meaning _____ _____ _____ _____

2 Split these words into two word families. Write the words in the answer boxes. Write the root word for each family.

useful   signature
usable   signpost   resign
signal   misuse   useless
signify   user

Root word _____

Root word _____

3 Write word families for these root words.

act _____

comfort _____

Give your child some different root words (e.g. bio, graph, log) and ask them to make word families for each one. Use a dictionary to check spellings and meanings.

Suffix 'ous'

Some words end in **ous**. **ous** at the end of a word often means **full of**.

ous is added when a word ends with a consonant.
peril   perilous
If a word ends with a silent **e**, remove the **e** before you add **ous**.
fame   famous
If a word ends in **our**, the **our** is changed to **or** before **ous** is added.
glamour   glamorous

1 Add **ous** to each of these words to make an adjective. You may need to change the ending of some of the words.

danger _____   joy _____   nerve _____

continue _____   poison _____   virtue _____

2 Write sentences for each of these adjectives.

famous _____

enormous _____

humorous _____

vigorous _____

dangerous _____

3 How many more words can you write that end in **ous**? Write them in the box.

Discuss with your child how the root word sometimes changes when a suffix is added. Find examples in your child's reading book and work out together what the root words are.

Words ending 'ious' and 'eous'

Sometimes **ious** or **eous** is added to a word.

ious is added when a word ends in **ion**, **y** or after a soft **c**.

rebell**ion**   rebell**ious**   var**y**   var**ious**   gra**ce**   gra**cious**

eous is added when a word ends in a soft **g**.

outra**ge**   outra**geous**

If the word ends in **e**, we need to delete the **e** before we add **ious** or **eous**.

spac**e**   spac**ious**   courag**e**   courag**eous**

1 Add **ious** or **eous** to each of these words to make an adjective.

religion _____   ambition _____   mystery _____

advantage _____   melody _____   malice _____

2 Write sentences about these different feelings.

> anxious   furious   envious   serious

I am _____ about _____

I am _____ about _____

I am _____ about _____

I am _____ about _____

3 How many more words can you write that end in **ious** and **eous**? Write them in the box.

Words ending 'sion' and 'tion'

The suffix **ion** usually has **s** or **t** in front of it.

deci**sion**   celebra**tion**

Words with **sion** or **tion** at the end make a **shun** sound.

When a verb has **ion** added to it, it often changes to a noun.

decide   deci**sion**   celebrate   celebra**tion**
(verb)   (noun)   (verb)   (noun)

1 Add **sion** or **tion** to make a word.

inven_____   expan_____   injec_____   exten_____

ac_____   hesita_____   comprehen_____ ten_____

2 Change these verbs into nouns by adding **sion** or **tion**. You may need to change the endings of some of the words first.

Verb	Noun	Verb	Noun
infect		intrude	
divide		imagine	
protect		concentrate	

3 Write three words ending in **sion** or **tion** in the boxes.
Use words that do not appear on this page.
Then put each word you have written into a sentence.

Prefixes 'bi', 'semi', 'tri' and 'oct'

bi, **semi**, **tri** and **oct** are prefixes.

bicycle   **semi**circle   **tri**angle   **oct**agon

bi means two   **semi** means half   **tri** means three   **oct** means eight

Some **semi** and **bi** words have a hyphen after the prefix.

semi-detached   **bi**-weekly

1 What am I? The answers are all words with **bi**, **semi**, **tri** or **oct** prefixes.

I am a bike with three wheels. _____

I am an eight-sided shape. _____

I am a sea creature with eight tentacles. _____

I am the match in a competition that comes before the final. _____

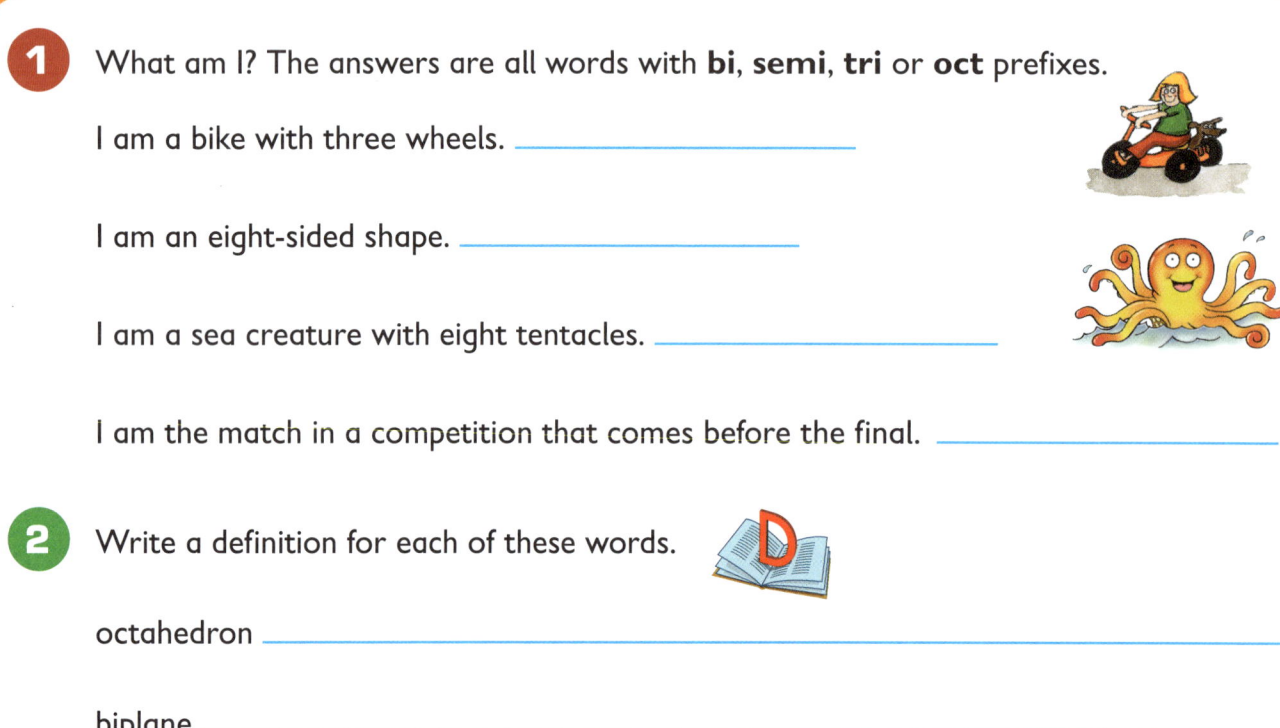

2 Write a definition for each of these words.

octahedron _____

biplane _____

tripod _____

3 Think of words to complete this table.

bi words	**semi** words	**tri** words	**oct** words

There are other numerical prefixes that your child could explore, for example, mono, hemi/demi, quart, dec.

Words ending 'ssion' and 'cian'

ion and **ian** are suffixes.

When they become **ssion** or **cian** at the end of a word, they make a **shun** sound.

If the verb ends in **ss** or **t**, the noun will be spelt with **ss**.
suppre**ss**   suppre**ssion**   permi**t**   permi**ssion**

If you hear the word **mission** inside the word, it will be spelt with **ss**.

cian words are often the names of jobs or hobbies.

electri**cian**   musi**cian**

1 Turn these verbs into nouns using the word ending **ssion**.

Verb	Noun	Verb	Noun
discuss		permit	
omit		possess	
progress		impress	

2 Make **cian** words from these root words. Check that you have spelt the finished words correctly.

Root word	**cian** word	Root word	**cian** word
mathematics		optic	
magic		electric	
politics		beauty	

3 Complete these sentences with **ssion** or **cian** words.

We lost many of our prized _____ in the fire.

The _____ played lots of my favourite songs.

We needed an _____ to re-wire our house.

The speaker made a big _____ on his audience.

Words ending 'cious' and 'tious'

Some adjectives end in **cious** and **tious**.

vi**cious**   infec**tious**

If the root word ends in **ce**, the adjective ends **cious**.   vi**ce**   vi**cious**

If the root word ends in **tion**, the adjective ends in **tious**.   cau**tion**   cau**tious**

Take care! Look at this exception.   conscien**ce**   conscien**tious**

Learn how to spell these tricky **cious** and **tious** words.

suspi**cious**   deli**cious**   face**tious**   scrump**tious**

1. Add **cious** or **tious** to these words to make new words. Make sure you spell the finished words correctly.

space _____   ambition _____

nutrition _____   grace _____

repetition _____   malice _____

infection _____   superstition _____

2. Write definitions for these words. Check your definitions in a dictionary.

suspicious _____

scrumptious _____

3. Choose a **cious** word and a **tious** word and write them in two sentences.

_____

_____

Give your child an oral spelling test using both the words on this page and also on page 29 to ensure that they can spell the words correctly.

Tricky words

Some tricky words just need to be learnt. Here are some helpful ways to remember them.

1 What do these pictures show? Write any you get wrong in the box.

c_____e   m_____e   q_____r

e_____e   i_____d   e_____h

2 Say each of these words out loud. Then cover it and write it in the space.

probably _____   peculiar _____   possession _____

occasionally _____   disappear _____   century _____

3 Identify the tricky part of the spelling of each of these words. Write a tip to help you to remember how to spell it.

For example, separate — There's a rat in sep-a-rat-e.

strength _____

caught _____

enough _____

With your child, make a 'personal dictionary' of tricky words. Write the words on notes and stick them around the house, or write the words in the air. This can help to fix the shape of the word in your child's memory.

Answers

Page 4
'ch' words

1 chicken, school, sandwich, choir

2
ch as in stomach	ch as in chin
technology	research
orchestra	chocolate
chemist	change

3 Child's own choice of nouns.

Page 5
More 'ch' words

1
ch as in chemistry	ch as in chalet
scheme	machine
ache	brochure
echo	chef

2 chauffeur, parachute, moustache, chef, quiche

3 Child's own sentences.

Page 6
Prefixes 're' and 'pre'

1 refresh—to give new strength / energy

return—to come / go back to a place

prearrange—arrange in advance

prehistoric—belonging to a time before written history

replace—to put something back / to change something

preschool—a nursery / kindergarten

2 reheat, preheat; retest, pretest; repay, prepay; rebook, prebook

3 Child's own choice of words.

Page 7
Prefixes 'aero', 'aqua' and 'tele'

1 aeroplane or aquaplane, aerospace, telephone, telegraph

2 Child's own sentences.

3 Definitions could be:
A small airport or airfield.
A cylinder full of air that divers use to breathe.
A viewing device that makes objects appear nearer.

Page 8
Prefixes 'inter', 'micro' and 'sub'

1 interview, subheadings, microscope

2 Child's own choice of words and sentences.

3 microchip, subterranean, intersect (✓)
interscope, microsect, subreact (✗)

Page 9
Possessive apostrophe with plural words

1 lynxes' territory, Mrs Henderson's daughters, the Jensens' house

2 Finches', Sanchezes

3 children's, parents', women's
Child's own sentences using children's, parents', women's

Page 10
Letter pattern 'sc'

1 scissors, scientific, fascinate, ascend, discipline

2
sc as in scare	sc as in science
biscuit	scent
score	scene
scrapbook	crescent
disco	muscle
scooter	scenery

3 Child's own sentences.

Page 11
Words with 'ey', 'ei' and 'eigh'

1 grey, reins, neighbour, survey, obey, weight

2 convey, freight, neigh, sleigh, grey (✓)
wiegh, weigh; vayl, veil; eyty, eighty; preigh, pray (✗)

3 Child's own words.

Page 12
Words ending 'ice' and 'ise'

1 exercise, surprise, realise, office

2 Child's own sentences.

3 paradise, cowardice, police, justice, organise, recognise

Page 13
Homophones

1 pair, pear; hare, hair; see, sea; paws, pause

2 main, weather, stake, who's
Child's own sentences.

3 they're, their; reign, rein; he'll, heal; sees, seas

Page 14
Words ending 'able' and 'ible'

1 comfortable, terrible, reasonable, sensible, visible, flexible, acceptable, possible

2 Child's own sentences.

3 inedible, reliable, comfortable, valuable

Page 15
Words ending 'ably' and 'ibly'

1
l	e	g	i	b	l	y	r	b	l	e	y
a	n	y	s	e	n	s	i	b	l	y	o
c	o	n	s	i	d	e	r	a	b	l	y
p	r	a	d	o	r	a	b	l	y	l	g
v	t	e	r	r	i	b	l	y	n	b	t
n	o	t	i	c	e	a	b	l	y	c	s
c	o	m	f	o	r	t	a	b	l	y	y
b	t	f	l	e	x	i	b	l	y	u	m

2 Child's own words and sentences.

3 responsibly, comfortably, considerably, reasonably

Page 16
Suffixes that start with a vowel

1 limiting, beginner, preferred, limitation, offered, permitted, upsetting, travelled

2 jeweler, jeweller; happening, happening; canceled, cancelled; fullfilled, fulfilled

3 Child's own sentences.

Page 17
Compound words

1 overhead, raindrop, afternoon, sunlight, pillowcase, handshake

2 backup, household, meatballs, newsletter, playground, password